The Friendly Dolphins

by PATRICIA LAUBER

Illustrated with Photographs

With drawings and diagrams by WILLIAM BARTLETT

Cover photo by MARINELAND OF FLORIDA

SCHOLASTIC BOOK SERVICES

NEW YORK • LONDON • RICHMOND HILL, ONTARIO

The author and publisher wish to thank F. G. Wood, Jr., Curator, Marine Studios, Marineland, Florida, for his assistance in the preparation of this book. Grateful acknowledgment is also made to Robert A. Dahne, Director of Public Relations at Marine Studios, for his help in obtaining many of the photographs.

A special edition of this book in a reinforced binding for school and library use is available directly from Random House School and Library Service, Inc., 457 Madison Avenue, New York, New York 10022. In addition, this book is also available in a hardcover edition through your local bookstore.

3rd printing. . . . . September 1968

Contents

The dolphin is the only creature who loves man for his own sake. Some land animals avoid man altogether, and the tame ones, such as dogs and horses, are tame because he feeds them . . . . The dolphin alone . . . has no need of any man, yet it is a genial friend to all and has helped many.

PLUTARCH, *a writer of ancient Greece*

A Friend
in the Sea

ONCE there was a boy named Dionysios, who lived long ago in Greece. He was just like any other boy. He had a home and family. He went to school each morning and played with his friends when school was out. We know about Dionysios for only one reason — a dolphin chose him as a friend. It happened this way.

On warm afternoons, Dionysios went to the beach. One day, while he was swimming, a dolphin came up to him. At first Dionysios was frightened. The dolphin was much bigger than he was, and its mouth was full of sharp teeth. But soon he realized that the dolphin meant him no harm. It wanted to play. Losing his fear, Dionysios played with it.

The next day Dionysios went back to the beach. The dolphin was waiting for him. Again they played together. And so it went. Day after day the dolphin was waiting for the boy, and the two became fast friends. Often the dolphin took Dionysios on its back. It carried him out to sea and then brought him safe to shore.

Word of what was happening spread far and wide. Crowds of people visited the beach to see the boy and his dolphin friend. And the story was written down. That is how we know about Dionysios, though he lived nearly 2,000 years ago.

Ancient writings are full of stories about dolphins. Here is one that took place near what is today Naples, Italy. It tells of a dolphin that lived in a salt-water lake. Near the same lake there lived a poor boy. Every day he walked around the lake to reach his school. During these walks he became friends with the dolphin. He could call it, and it would come. He fed it. Soon each lost fear of the other.

One morning the boy stepped into the water and

Ancient peoples used the graceful dolphin as decoration. *Left:* A Greek coin over 2,000 years old. *Below:* A carved Greek gem.

climbed onto the dolphin's back. The dolphin carried him across the lake to school. After that, the dolphin took the boy to school every morning and brought him home at night.

About the same time, there was in North Africa a town called Hippo. The boys of Hippo spent all their free time in the sea. One day a boy was swimming far out from shore. A dolphin joined him. It swam all around him. It dove under him and took him on its back. It rolled him into the sea. Then the dolphin again took the boy on its back. It rode him out to sea, turned, and carried him back to shore.

For several days the dolphin appeared when the boys went swimming. Each time the boys fled. Each time the dolphin seemed to invite them to stay. It leaped and dove in the way that dolphins play.

The men of Hippo had come to watch the dolphin. After a while they began to feel ashamed. Why should anyone fear this friendly dolphin? They called to it. They went near it. They touched it. Since the dolphin seemed to like being touched, they stroked it.

Now the boys became braver and swam near the dolphin. Among them was the boy who had first met the dolphin. He swam next to it. He climbed on its back and was taken for a ride. After that, the boy and dolphin often played together.

Many people came to see the friendly dolphin of Hippo. And this story, too, was written down.

It is clear that ancient Romans and Greeks knew many dolphins and liked them. We find dolphins on old coins. We find them carved in gems. We find them in wall paintings. Most of all, we find them in poems, stories, and histories.

Some of the dolphin tales are made up. They could not have happened. But other tales tell how dolphins played arounds ships; how they helped fishermen by driving fish into their nets; how they saved the lives of people who were drowning. These stories are probably true, for dolphins do the same things today.

Dolphins often accompany ships, sporting and racing around them. They ride the waves made by a ship's bows.

Dolphins still help fishermen. And fishermen know the dolphins are their friends. They share their catch with the dolphins that have herded fish into the nets.

Dolphins have saved the lives of people who were drowning. A few years ago, a woman was swimming in Florida. She was caught by a strong current and could not fight her way out of it. She had given up hope when something suddenly gave her a great shove onto the beach. Looking back, she saw a dolphin leaping and playing in the water. A man on the beach told her that the dolphin had pushed her ashore.

The dolphin may simply have been playing. No one can tell. But it did save the woman's life. And other dolphins have saved other lives.

Do dolphins make friends with children? Were those ancient tales of boys and dolphins true? It seemed doubtful. No such thing had taken place in modern times. Then, in 1955, it did happen. A wild dolphin made friends with another child.

This time it happened in New Zealand, near the town of Opononi. A dolphin came into the harbor and swam near the fishing boats. The fishermen found that she liked to be scratched with an oar. The dolphin, whom the men named Opo, grew bolder. She followed the boats in and began to play among the swimmers.

Opo was willing to play with grownups. But she preferred children. She chose to swim among them, making clear that she wanted to be petted. And Opo picked one as her special friend. This was a 13-year-old girl named Jill Baker. If Jill swam off, Opo followed. Several times

A boy swimming with a friendly dolphin

the dolphin swam between Jill's legs, picked her up, and gave her a short ride. She would come to Jill for rubbing and petting. She even let Jill put small children on her back.

Like all dolphins, Opo loved to play. Someone gave her a colored beach ball. Opo soon invented a game with it. She tossed it into the air with her head. Then she rushed to the place where it was going to fall and tossed it into the air again. Sometimes she tossed the ball into the air and batted it with her tail.

When people laughed or clapped, Opo seemed pleased. She leaped gaily out of the water. But she was always careful not to leap near people. For dolphins are gentle with their human friends. If someone was rough with Opo, she simply swam away, slapping her tail on the water.

As the year passed, more and more people came to see Opo. Sometimes as many as 1,500 came on a Saturday or a Sunday.

Then, in March, 1956, Opo vanished. When the fishermen found her, she was dead. Somehow she had become trapped in a rocky pool when the water went out. All over New Zealand, people grieved for the friendly dolphin. She was buried at Opononi, and her grave was covered with flowers.

Opo had proved that dolphins do make friends with children. This is a rare thing, but it does happen.

Dolphins show a liking for man.

Many other dolphins have shown a liking for people. Free and wild, they have chosen to come near people. They have given every sign of liking human company. Almost no other creature of the sea does such a thing. And on land it is usually tame animals who are friends with us.

So that is one reason why many people are interested in dolphins — they seem to like us. But there are other reasons, too, because dolphins are remarkable animals. For instance, though they live in the sea, dolphins are not fish. They are mammals.

Mammals in the Sea

A DOLPHIN looks more like a fish than certain fishes do. It has a smooth, streamlined body. It is an excellent swimmer. As its powerful tail moves up and down, the dolphin seems to flash through the water. Like fish, dolphins are completely at home in the water. There they play, feed, sleep, and bear their young. Dolphins live in the water and can live only in the water. Yet they are not fish.

If you watch a dolphin, you will see something that shows it is not a fish. A dolphin must come to the surface to breathe. Fish can take oxygen out of the water. Dolphins cannot. Like us, they breathe with lungs and must take their oxygen from the air. And like us, they are mammals.

Mammals are a large class of animals with backbones. Mammals nurse their young on milk. They are warm-

Unlike fish, dolphins must surface to breathe.

blooded. Almost all mammals bear living young. And most of them have hair. Dogs, cats, horses, cows, pigs, mice, monkeys, and bats are all mammals. We are mammals. So are dolphins and their close relatives, the whales and porpoises.

Dolphins belong to a family that scientists call the

Cetacea.[1] The family has two main branches.

One branch is made up of the world's giant whales. The scientific name for them is Mysticeti,[2] which means "mustache whales." Mustache whales do not have teeth. Rather, they have something like a huge mustache inside their mouths. This is baleen, or whalebone. The big whales strain their food out of the sea through the baleen.

The other main branch of the family is made up of Odontoceti,[3] which means "toothed whales." There is only one giant in this branch of the family — the sperm whale. The other members are small whales, dolphins, and porpoises.

Dolphins and porpoises are much alike. In fact, they are so much alike that there is only one sure way to tell them apart. That is by the shape of their teeth. Porpoises have spade-shaped teeth. Dolphins have cone-shaped teeth.

Because dolphins and porpoises are alike, many people call all of them porpoises. (A second reason is that there is a large fish also named dolphin.) Other people prefer to use both names — porpoise and dolphin.

There are many kinds of dolphins in the seas. Among the best known is the bottle-nose dolphin. This dolphin lives along coasts. So it is a familiar dolphin and one that scientists have studied closely. This book is mostly about the bottle-nose.

[1]Say: see-TAY-shee ah. [2]Say: MISS-tih-SEE-tee. [3]Say: oh-DON-toe-SEE-tee.

THE DOLPHIN AND SOME RELATIVES

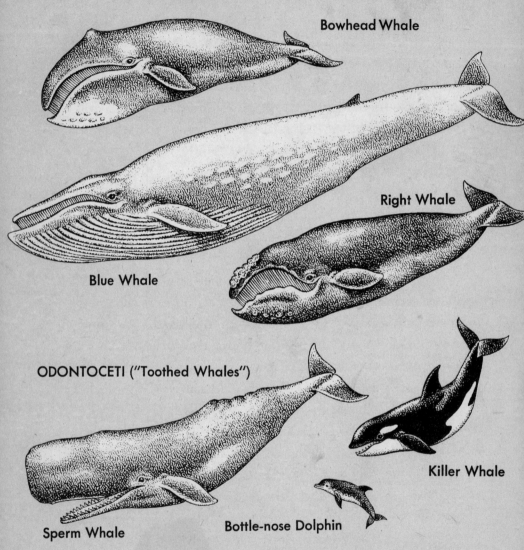

MYSTICETI ("Mustache Whales")

Bowhead Whale

Blue Whale

Right Whale

ODONTOCETI ("Toothed Whales")

Sperm Whale

Bottle-nose Dolphin

Killer Whale

Dolphins are whales. This family has two branches: "Mustache Whales" and "Toothed Whales." Here are some members of both branches, showing how they compare with each other in size.

A bottle-nose dolphin may be 7 to 11 feet long and weigh 300 to 700 pounds. The easiest way to tell a bottle-nose is by its mouth. When the mouth is closed, a bottle-nose appears to be smiling. This is not a real smile, but just a curve of the mouth. The curving mouth gives the dolphin a friendly look. And bottle-noses are friendly. It was a bottle-nose that made friends with Jill Baker in New Zealand.

Like all Cetacea, dolphins are mammals of the sea. Most mammals are land animals. So perhaps it is not surprising to learn that dolphins and their relatives are descended from land animals. Long ago, dolphin ancestors left the land for the sea.

We do not know why this happened. But we do know that it happened 50 to 60 million years ago. At that time the earth was very different from the earth we know today. The land was different. Animals and plants were different. And there were no men on earth.

Among the animals was a kind that would become the dolphin we know.

No one is sure exactly what kind of animal it was. But there is reason to think it was related to grass-eating animals like the cow. Modern dolphins are fish-eaters. Yet their stomachs are like those of animals that eat plants. Their blood is also like that of grazing animals.

Nor is anyone sure what this early animal looked like. It may have looked a little like a pig — with four short legs, some hair, and a head that came out into a snout. Set in the head were two small ears, two eyes, a nose, and a mouth.

The animal's tail was probably like an otter's — thick and strong at the base.

For some reason, this animal was drawn toward the water. It was drawn toward swamps, rivers, and the sea, where it searched for food. Perhaps it was driven there by bigger, fiercer animals. We do not know. But dolphin ancestors began to spend more and more time in the water. The result was that the animal form began to change.

Bottle-nose dolphins appear to be smiling.

This does not mean that any one animal changed. It means that the form of the animals changed over a very long time.

The easiest way to understand what happened is to take a different example. Suppose a farmer wants short-legged sheep because they are easier to fence in. He selects the sheep with the shortest legs and breeds them. Their lambs tend to have short legs. Later he breeds the short-legged lambs and gets more lambs with even shorter legs. This way he can develop a race of short-legged sheep.

In the example, a man did the selecting. But such selecting also takes place in nature. It is called *natural selection*. It works this way. Among animals of a kind, some do better than others. They are better fitted for life. In time, they come to be the only animals of their kind. The others have died out.

That is what happened with the dolphins.

The dolphin ancestors were not all alike. Some were better fitted for life in the water than others. Perhaps they were slightly more streamlined in shape; this is helpful for moving through water. Perhaps they had stronger tails; stronger tails are helpful for swimming.

So certain dolphin ancestors were more successful in the water. They swam better than the others. This meant that they caught more food and had fewer accidents. They lived longer and so had more young. The young tended to be like their parents.

Another "toothed whale"—the pilot whale

Little by little, the animal becames the dolphin of today.

Here are just a few of the changes that took place.

The dolphin ancestor had four legs. But legs are not very helpful in the water. The modern dolphin has no legs. The front legs have become flippers, which are useful for steering. The flipper is a mitten of flesh. Inside, though, are the bones of a leg and foot. Hind legs were not needed at all. Only a trace of them remains. The dolphin skeleton has two bones that were once hip bones.

Hair does not help a mammal that lives only in the sea. Dolphins no longer have hair on their bodies. (Only one trace of hair remains. Baby dolphins are born with a few bristly hairs on their snouts. These hairs soon fall out.)

Dolphins today are perfectly suited to a life in the sea.

The dolphin shape is now as streamlined as it can be. The tail is big, broad, and strong.

The dolphin head has also changed. The head is drawn out into a beak with a large mouth — a fine fish-catcher. The nose has become a blowhole on top of the head. This makes it easier for a dolphin to breathe when it comes up for air. Dolphins still have ears, but all that can be seen is a tiny pinhole. The outside ear has disappeared. It is no help in the water.

With these changes, the mammal dolphin has become perfectly suited to a life in the sea.

BOTTLE-NOSE DOLPHIN

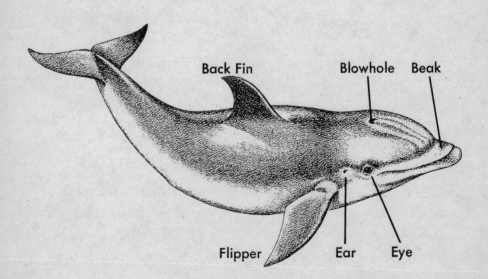

Back Fin   Blowhole   Beak

Flipper   Ear   Eye

Dolphin
Life

DOLPHINS are very fast swimmers. We know this because they like to play around ships and boats. A playing dolphin can keep up with a ship traveling at 25 miles an hour. This is not a dolphin's top speed. A dolphin can swim faster underwater. There, waves do not drag at its body and slow it down. Then too, a dolphin in a hurry probably swims faster than a dolphin at play. So far there is no way of finding out just how fast a dolphin can swim. But what we know shows that dolphins are among the sea's fastest swimmers.

A dolphin does not swim the way a fish does. A fish, like a snake, moves by bending its backbone sideways. A fish flicks its way through the water. A dolphin has a backbone that bends up and down. So the dolphin's broad, strong tail moves up and down. This moving tail

A dolphin keeping pace with a speeding motor boat

drives the dolphin forward. The dolphin steers with its flippers and with twists of its tail.

A dolphin can turn as quickly as a fish. Because of its mammal backbone, it can do what a fish cannot do: move quickly up or down. With a few strokes of its tail, a dolphin can shoot to the surface. This is very important. For dolphins are mammals. They must surface to breathe.

A dolphin surfaces with a smooth, rolling movement. All you see is its back curving above the surface. The back flashes into sight, then vanishes. This short time is enough to let the dolphin breathe.

Breathing is done through the blowhole on top of

the dolphin's head. The blowhole leads to the windpipe. And the windpipe leads to the lungs.

As a dolphin arches through the air, it breathes very quickly. It blows out the used air and draws in fresh air. The blowhole snaps shut. And the dolphin disappears under the water.

With filled lungs, a dolphin can stay underwater for four to six minutes. This amount of time allows freedom of movement in the water.

A dolphin steers with its flippers and tail.

No one knows how wild dolphins sleep. But dolphins at aquariums sleep in short catnaps by day and by night. Sometimes they sleep floating about a foot below the surface of the water. When they need to breathe, a stroke of the tail brings them up. A sleeping dolphin can surface without waking, just as we can roll over.

Dolphins can also sleep while swimming. They swim slowly, rising to breathe two or three times a minute. Their eyes may be closed or partly open.

One thing that helps support a sleeping dolphin is the layer of blubber, or fat, beneath its skin. Blubber buoys up a dolphin and helps keep it afloat.

Dolphins asleep underwater

The blubber also serves in other ways. It helps make dolphins streamlined. And it keeps their body heat from escaping too fast. This is important because dolphins, being mammals, are warm-blooded.

Many animals, such as fishes and snakes, are cold-blooded. The term does not mean that their blood is icy cold. It means that the body temperature of the animal is the same as the temperature around it. A fish's temperature is low in cold water; it is high in warm water. A snake's temperature is high in the sun; it is low in a cool cave.

In a warm-blooded animal, body temperature always stays about the same. Your temperature is always about 98.6 degrees; it never changes by more than a few degrees. A dolphin's body temperature also stays the same; it stays the same in warm water and in cool water.

If you touched a dolphin in cool water, you would notice two things. You would find that the outside of its body was cool. But the breath from the blowhole would be warm, because the dolphin is warm inside.

The heat of a warm-blooded animal comes from its food. The body changes food into energy, much of which is heat. To keep an even temperature, the body both makes heat and gives off heat.

In cold air or water, the body must have a way of guarding its heat. Otherwise it would give off more heat than it could make.

Most mammals are covered with hair or fur. This thick covering guards their body heat and keeps it from escaping too fast. We are not covered with hair. So we cover ourselves with clothing.

Dolphins long ago lost their hair. It did not keep them warm in the water. They developed instead their layer of blubber. The blubber is a covering that slows down the escape of heat.

In that way, warm-blooded dolphins have become suited to life where hair would not help them. This kind of change is called *adaptation*.

Still another kind of adaptation is even more astounding. Most mammals, you remember, bear living young and nurse them on milk. This is what dolphins do — underwater.

Like all dolphins, the Pacific white-sided dolphin has a layer of blubber under its skin.

Baby Dolphins

BABY BIRDS hatch out of eggs. So do most baby fishes and snakes. But almost all baby mammals are born in a different way. They are carried inside their mothers' bodies until they are ready to be born.

Some baby mammals are born helpless. Kittens cannot see and cannot walk. Human babies cannot walk either; nor can they take care of themselves in any way.

The young of horses and cows are different. Horses and cows are grazing animals that must move to find food. Their young are born able to see and to run beside their mothers.

In bearing young, dolphins are like cows and horses. A mother dolphin does not have a litter of baby dolphins. She bears one baby. Her baby is not so helpless as a kitten. It is born able to see and to swim.

A helpless baby could not survive in the ocean. A newborn dolphin must be able to surface for air at once.

It must be able to swim with its mother. There is no way a mother dolphin could hide and guard a helpless baby.

For many years not much was known about dolphin mothers and babies. It was almost impossible to study wild ones. But recently some aquariums have been raising dolphins in big salt-water tanks. There scientists have been able to study them.

We now know that a mother dolphin carries her baby for 12 months. During the second half of that year, she begins to spend more time by herself. She chooses a special female friend. The friend later acts as an "aunt," who helps with the baby.

The birth of a dolphin takes from a few minutes to two hours. And a baby is usually born tail first. Most baby mammals are born head first, but they are born on dry land. Dolphins are born underwater. Here a baby would drown if it tried to breathe before it was free of its mother. This may be why baby dolphins are born tail first.

As the birth begins, other dolphins gather round the mother. They guard her against danger. For instance, they keep sharks away. If a shark approaches, they either chase it or butt it in the gills and kill it.

The moment the baby is free, it swims to the surface for a breath of air. The mother and the "aunt" follow. If the baby needs help, the mother pushes it with her snout.

A baby dolphin is born tail first.

A newborn dolphin looks just like its mother, except that it is smaller. Three feet long, it weighs about 25 pounds. Its eyes are open, and it can see. It hears clearly. A baby soon learns to recognize its mother's call and to "talk" with whistles and grunts. A baby dolphin lacks only teeth. They take several weeks to cut through the gums.

The mother dolphin feeds her baby on milk. The milk comes from two glands set near her tail. And here is another way that dolphins differ from land mammals.

As its mother squirts out milk, the baby feeds.

On land, babies get their milk by sucking. Underwater, sucking would be almost impossible. So a baby dolphin does not have to suck. The mother has a special set of muscles. By tightening these, she can squirt out milk. In this way, the baby can easily feed. It gets a gulp of milk, goes to the surface for air, and comes back for more milk.

A young dolphin at first stays close to its mother. Usually it swims beside the fin on her back. Often the "aunt" swims with the mother and baby. The mother dolphin keeps a watchful eye on her baby. She does not allow it to swim away from her.

Later the mother gives the baby more freedom. But the baby does not leave her until it is about 18 months old. By this time it has stopped nursing and is eating only solid food.

Dolphins eat small fish, such as mullet, butterfish,

A young dolphin stays close to its mother until it is about a year and a half old.

Adult dolphins eat fish.

herring, and sea trout. A full-grown dolphin eats about
20 pounds of fish a day.

A dolphin has many teeth. For example, a young
bottle-nose has 80 to 100, all the same shape and size.
Cone-shaped and sharp, they curve backward a little.
They are well suited to their work. A dolphin uses its
mouth and teeth only for catching fish. A fish is crushed
between the teeth and swallowed whole.

A wild dolphin may hunt fish alone. But often dolphins work together as a team. They surround a school of fish and herd it into shallow water. Each dolphin in turn goes in to feed. The others keep the fish trapped.

In aquariums, dolphins are fed by their keepers. That is how we know about their eating habits.

We have also learned many other things from aquarium dolphins. One is that young dolphins are very playful. They are as playful as puppies, kittens, or human babies. Another is that dolphins are very intelligent.

Dolphins are both playful and intelligent.

Play and Intelligence

DOLPHINS are quick learners who enjoy doing tricks. Perhaps you have seen dolphins doing tricks at a big aquarium, such as the one at Marineland, Florida. Or you may have seen dolphins on TV. Dolphins have been taught to "shake hands" with their flippers, blow horns, and leap through hoops. They have learned to leap out of the water, grasp ropes in their mouths, and ring dinner bells.

Marineland dolphins enjoy playing basketball, passing the ball among themselves. Several have become very good at making baskets. They toss the ball through a hoop mounted five feet above the water. Flippy, a Marineland favorite, can make two baskets in a row more than half of the time.

Flippy is also the star of the baseball game that dolphins play. He pitches, "argues" noisily with the "um-

Leaping through a hoop

pire," and fields the batted ball to put the "runner" out.

Young dolphins also enjoy playing by themselves and inventing games. The men at Marineland tell many stories of how dolphins amuse themselves. For example, Priscilla played with a turtle. She balanced it on her snout. She also gave it rides around the tank.

Young dolphins are great teasers. They enjoy pestering the other animals that live in their tank.

One dolphin took to teasing a fish. The fish was trying to swim forward. The dolphin kept taking it by the tail and pulling it backward. Each time, the dolphin let the fish go. The fish hurried away. Then the dolphin again grasped its tail and pulled the fish backward.

A dolphin named Algae enjoyed teasing a red grouper (which is a large fish). The grouper lived in a cave of rocks. Algae would take a piece of squid and lay it outside the mouth of the cave. Then he would back off and wait. As soon as the grouper came out to eat the squid, Algae snatched it away.

The same dolphin invented a fine game for himself. He played it with a pelican feather. Algae carried the feather to the bottom of the tank. There jets of sea water poured into the tank, making currents. When Algae let the feather go, it was carried away in the current. Algae

Playing basketball

chased it, caught it, and took it back to the jet. Later Algae played this game with another dolphin. One took the feather to the jet. The other waited to chase it.

All dolphins like to play with an inner tube. They soon learn to throw the tube just where they want it to go. Algae was excellent at this game. While still very young, he had learned to hurl the tube right out of the tank. He found that if he did this, someone would throw the tube back. This made a splendid game.

Dolphin games are fun for the dolphins. They are fun for the people who watch. But they are also of interest to scientists. For the games tell something about the intelligence of dolphins. They seem to show that dolphins are among the most intelligent of mammals. Dolphins are probably as intelligent as dogs. They may be as intelligent as chimpanzees. This means that they rank high among the mammals. Chimps are ranked second to man himself.

Animal intelligence is never easy to measure. And it is very hard to measure in an animal that lives in the water. Scientists cannot give a dolphin the same tests that they give to chimps. They must study dolphins in other ways.

One way is to study the dolphin brain. It is a large brain. The thinking part is big. This is one sign that dolphins may be highly intelligent.

Other signs are found in dolphin behavior.

Priscilla giving a ride to a favorite turtle

For example, teasing is a sign of intelligence. Teasing is action taken on purpose. The teaser expects something to happen because of his action. That is, he thinks ahead. Only the higher, more intelligent animals think ahead.

Dolphins can invent games. They can learn games from each other. And they learn quickly. They play games for half an hour or more. They can make changes in the way a game is played. All these things are signs of high intelligence.

Another sign is the ability to solve problems. And dolphins are good at solving problems.

Dolphins playing with an inner tube

One day a Marineland dolphin was playing with a wet pelican feather. She was throwing it to a human friend. On one throw the feather did not clear the tank. It stuck to the wall, above the water level. How could the dolphin free the feather?

She solved the problem this way. She rose out of the water and wiped the feather off with the side of her head. Then she picked it up and went on with the game.

Two scientists reported this example of dolphin behavior. They saw a pair of bottle-noses teasing an eel. The eel was in a crack in a rock. The dolphins were trying to pull it out. They could get at the eel. They could pull it back and forth between them. But they could not get it out. After a while, one bottle-nose swam off. It came back with a newly killed scorpion fish, which has very sharp spines. The dolphin poked the eel with the scorpion fish. The eel popped out of the crack. The dolphins caught it, took it to the middle of the tank, and let it go.

This dolphin has been taught to leap over a bar.

Scientists never pretend to know what an animal is thinking. So these men did not try to explain what happened with the eel. But it looked like a good piece of problem-solving.

Feelings, or emotions, are another sign of a higher animal. A higher animal has feeling for other animals of its kind. It forms close attachments. We do this. So do dogs and chimps. Lower animals, like rats, do not.

Dolphins do have such feelings. Mother and young are closely attached. Some dolphins become close friends and stay close friends. When a friend or mate dies, a dolphin shows signs of sorrow. It may circle the body, making a whistling noise. It may even refuse to eat.

Dolphins also help one another. This, too, is a sign of a higher animal. For example, once an underwater explosion went off near a school of bottle-noses. One dolphin was stunned. Quickly, two others swam up. Each placed its head under a flipper to keep the stunned dolphin afloat. In a few minutes he recovered. Then, and only then, the whole school swam off.

For all these reasons, scientists feel sure dolphins rank among the higher animals. They feel sure dolphins are very intelligent.

One scientist is making a special study of dolphin brains and intelligence. His name is John C. Lilly. His work may tell us much about dolphin intelligence.

Dolphins form close friendships among themselves.

Dr. Lilly also has another interest in dolphins. He thinks that someday he may be able to talk with them. He is trying to understand the noises dolphins make. And he is trying to teach them English.

Dolphins make many kinds of whistling and grunting noises. These noises are a kind of dolphin talk. They may show that a dolphin is excited, pleased, or sad. Mothers call their babies by whistling. Dolphins whistle to keep in touch when they are swimming around.

Dr. Lilly thinks that the grunts and whistles are a language. He is recording the noises and studying them. He hopes to understand the language.

There is much to be learned about dolphin talk. But most scientists do not think dolphins talk in words. They think the noises may be more like the barks, howls, and growls of a dog. A dog has many ways of telling you what he wants or how he feels. But this is not the same as using words.

Could dolphins learn to use words? Could they learn to speak English? Dr. Lilly thinks this may be possible. He records on tape all the noises that his dolphins make. Among these noises are some that sound like English words. He believes his dolphins are mimicking what they hear.

This may well be so; but it is still not the same as talking English, other scientists point out. For example, parrots are excellent mimics. Yet they cannot use words to say what they think or feel.

Everyone agrees that it would be wonderful if dolphins could learn English. But only time will tell how Dr. Lilly's work comes out.

Meanwhile, other scientists have been studying dolphin sounds for a different reason. And they have made some very interesting discoveries.

Dolphin Sonar

THE SEA is a very noisy place. Its waters are alive with the noises of fishes, crabs, shrimps, and other sea creatures. A person sitting in a boat does not hear these noises. But scientists have a way of listening in. Their chief tool is the *hydrophone*. This is an underwater microphone. The sounds it picks up can be recorded on tape. Using it, scientists have recorded clicks, clacks, rattles, thumps, grunts, croaks, and other noises.

Dolphins are some of the noisiest sea dwellers. They are seldom still. They whistle through their blowholes. They clap their jaws together. They make noises that sound like squeaks, moans, mews, barks, clicks, creaks, and sputters.

Some years ago, scientists decided that many of these noises were dolphin talk. But the other noises were a puzzle. They had nothing to do with how a dol-

A scientist with an underwater microphone for recording dolphin sounds

phin was feeling. They had nothing to do with how dolphins keep in touch. What were they?

A second dolphin puzzle also interested scientists. This one had to do with how dolphins found their way through the water.

Dolphins could swim at top speed and never hit anything. They could find their way among ships, rocks, anchors, and docks. They could do this on the blackest of nights. They could do it in muddy or cloudy water. Dolphins seemed to be seeing at times when seeing was impossible. How did they do this?

It turned out that the first puzzle was the answer to the second. It turned out that dolphins "see" with their ears. This is what happens:

One kind of dolphin noise is made up of a series of rapid clicks. To our ears, the clicks run together. They make a rasping, creaking noise, like a door swinging on rusty hinges. To dolphin ears, the clicks do not run together. These are the noises they use for "seeing" with their ears.

A dolphin sends out a burst of clicks. The sounds travel through the water. When they hit a solid object, they bounce off it. They bounce back toward the dolphin. The dolphin hears the echoes. It hears them so well that it can tell solid things are near. It knows where they are. It knows what shape they are. It knows how big they are.

That is how dolphins avoid hitting the sea bottom. That is how they avoid rocks, floating objects, and each other. And that is how they find their food.

Dolphins are not the only animals that "see" with their ears. Shrews do it. So do bats. In fact, the first studies were made of bats. Scientists found that bats were using echoes to locate objects in their paths. So what the bats were doing was named *echo-location.*

Men also make use of echo-location. A blind man tapping his stick is making use of it. And two electronic inventions make use of it. One is *radar,* which sends out radio waves. The other is *sonar,* which sends out sound waves. Sonar is used under water, where radio waves do not work.

Dolphins' sensing of echoes is called either sonar or echo-location.

Several scientists have studied dolphin sonar. The longest study was made by Winthrop N. Kellogg.

Dr. Kellogg knew about bats and sonar. He wondered if dolphins also could sense echoes. He decided to find

out. He chose to study bottle-nose dolphins. Bottle-noses live chiefly along coasts. There the water is less clear than in the middle of the ocean. And there are more objects a dolphin must avoid. So the bottle-nose would need the best sonar — if dolphins had sonar.

Dr. Kellogg started with the rapid clicking noises that dolphins make. Were they like sonar signals? Could they be used to locate objects? The answer turned out to be yes.

Dr. Kellogg set up a laboratory in an outdoor pool. In the pool he placed two dolphins from Marineland. They were called Albert and Betty. (Albert turned out to be the star performer.) Then Dr. Kellogg began experiments that went on for six years.

There is not space to tell of all Dr. Kellogg's work. But here are six of his discoveries:

1. He found that the dolphins kept close "watch" on their pool. Every 15 to 20 seconds, they sent out a burst of clicking noises. In this way, they kept "glancing" around the pool.

2. Their hearing proved very keen. They heard the slightest sound. A single BB shot was tossed into the pool. Its small plunk brought on a burst of clicking. The shot quickly sank, and the clicking stopped. The same thing happened when half a teaspoonful of water was splashed into the pool.

3. Each time a fish was splashed into the pool, the dolphins swam toward it. It was clear they could tell

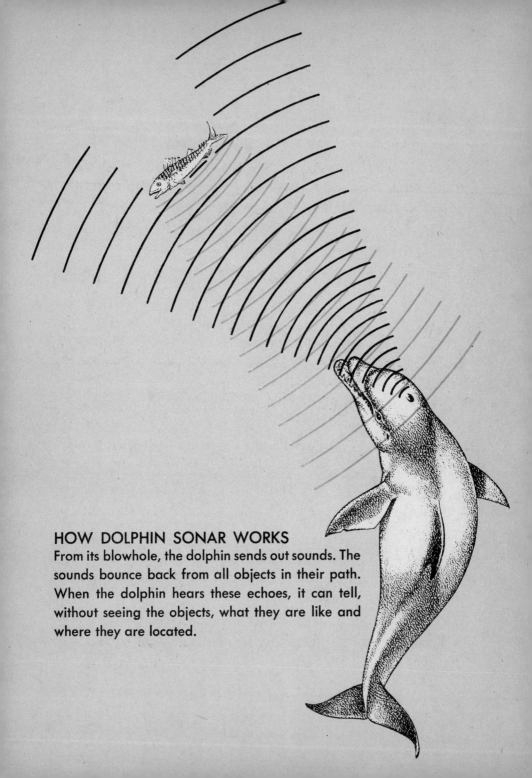

HOW DOLPHIN SONAR WORKS

From its blowhole, the dolphin sends out sounds. The sounds bounce back from all objects in their path. When the dolphin hears these echoes, it can tell, without seeing the objects, what they are like and where they are located.

what had been put in the water. If a fish was silently slipped in, Albert also found it at once.

4. How was Albert finding the fish? Dr. Kellogg thought Albert was using sonar. But perhaps Albert was using his eyes. Dr. Kellogg designed some tests to find out. Fish were slipped into the water on dark, moonless nights. With no light to see by, Albert still found the fish. In another kind of test, two fish were slipped into the water. One was simply in the water. The other was behind a sheet of clear glass; it could be seen, but it could not be found by sonar. In 202 tests, Albert never made a mistake. He never went after the fish behind glass. He always took the other. This showed he was not using his eyes to find fish.

5. Perhaps Albert was using his sense of taste. This did not seem likely. But a scientist must be sure. Dr. Kellogg set up a different kind of test. In it, food tastes would not help.

He divided the pool with a long steel net. The net had two openings in it. One was blocked by a sheet of clear glass. The other was open. Albert and Betty were then chased from one end of the pool to the other. Each dolphin was chased 50 times. From time to time, the glass was shifted from one opening to the other.

In the 100 trials, Albert and Betty made a total of two mistakes. Only twice did they try to swim through the glass. These tests showed that the dolphins had to be using sonar. They were swimming faster than usual. Yet they managed to find the right opening.

6. The last experiment was the most surprising. It showed that the dolphins could tell one fish from another by size.

Albert and Betty did not like mullet. They preferred a smaller fish called spot. So Dr. Kellogg worked out tests using mullet and spot. The mullet were 12 inches

Dr. Kellogg worked with Albert and Betty in a large outdoor pool.

long. The spot were 6 inches long. In the test, a mullet and a spot were lowered into the water at the same time.

The dolphins quickly learned to tell the difference by size. In his first 16 trials, Albert made four mistakes. In the next 140 trials, he made no mistakes. He picked the spot every time. He could find it in clear or muddy water, by day or by night.

Dr. Kellogg was certain that Albert's sonar told him which was the smaller fish. To be extra sure, he changed the test. Albert was offered a choice of a 6-inch spot or 6 inches of mullet. In these tests, Albert was wrong half of the time. When the fish were the same size, he could not tell one from another. Yet Albert's sonar could tell a 6-inch fish from a 12-inch fish.

Dr. Kellogg's findings were of great interest to scientists who study animals. They were also of interest to scientists who worked with sonar and to the United States Navy.

Dolphin sonar is much better than ours. Our sonar cannot tell a steel ship from a wooden one. It cannot always tell a whale from a submarine. Perhaps we can learn from dolphins how to improve our sonar.

There are many other things we need to know about the ocean world and about the animal world. Scientists are hoping to learn some of them from the gentle dolphins, our friends in the sea.

Photograph Credits: Annan Photo Features, page 28; Frank S. Essapian, 16; Robert Hermes, National Audubon Society, 36; Robert Kohler, 58; Marine Studios, 11, 27, 34, 35, 37; Marineland of the Pacific, 6, 42; Metropolitan Museum of Art, New York (gift of J. Pierpont Morgan, 1905), 8; Miami Seaquarium, 20, 38, 41; courtesy of Museum of Fine Arts, Boston, 8; Peter Stackpole (courtesy of *Life* magazine), 12, 22 23, 30, 44, 45, 46, 48, 50, 54, 59; U. S. Naval Ordance Test Station, Pasadena, California, 52; Werner Stoy, Camera Hawaii, 26.